THE TRIALS AND TRIUMPHS OF DOWN SYNDROME

by

Kelly Krei

October 10, 2007

Sometime back I was reading a newsletter provided by Parent to Parent of Colorado; the feature article by Jennifer Vasquez was titled "Nurturing Parent Involvement." In the opening paragraph, the author stated that an idea is somewhat like a seed. A seed blows in the wind and lands in dirt (peaks our interest), then the seed receives water and sunshine and, low and behold, the idea (the seed) begins to grow. At the end of her article the author plants her seed with the reader and her hope is that one day soon, the reader would take time to water that planted seed.

Further into the newsletter, I stopped on a book review that was submitted by a fellow reader. The title of the book being reviewed was *Married with Special Needs Children* written by Laura E. Marshak, Ph.D., published in 2007. The reader providing the review was the parent/caregiver of a six-year-old who had Smith-Magenis syndrome. In the review the reader stated that she was "mildly disappointed" in the book, stating that the book covered only the basics of how to maintain a relationship for "new" parents of a child born with a disability. However, what the reader was looking for was "real-life examples". Thus the seed was planted.

TABLE OF CONTENTS

INTRODUCTION

My wife, Michele, and I married June 16th, 1984, after a very long period of dating. We met in the summer of 1983, began dating in January of 1984 and on February 13th, 1984, I asked her to marry me. She had quickly become my second best friend. She had an amazing smile and beautiful eyes; she worked hard and was just generally fun to be with. My first best friend, my dad, liked her, as did my mother. Now, please do not go reading anything into my dad being my best friend and my mom just getting a mention; my dad and I had a great relationship as father and son and as friends, and though he left this earth long ago, he remains in my heart today.

Michele was born in 1962 and I in 1961, so you figure the math – when we married we were in our early 20's. This was my second marriage; I had married my high school sweetheart; due to a lack of maturity, that marriage ended shortly after it began.

Fortunately for me, Michele saw something in me that did not make her hesitate in accepting my proposal. Her parents were probably less thrilled with me than my parents were with her, due to the fact that I was divorced and they were Catholic. Regardless, they did see that their daughter and I had a tremendous chemistry and love for each other, and gave us their blessing.

We originally met during my senior year in high school; Michele was a junior and had just moved to my hometown, Worland, Wyoming, with her family from Pierre, South Dakota. Her parents both worked as medical professionals and had accepted positions at the local hospital. My first impression of Michele was that she was rather odd; she wore these bright, almost fluorescent, yellow boots, similar to the boots worn by fire fighters. Other than this, I really did not pay much attention to her, because as I stated earlier, I was hooked on someone else at the time.

From the time I graduated in 1979 until the summer of 1983, I had not seen, thought of, nor heard from Michele. My life during this time was spent living in Dallas, Texas, then Denver, Colorado, and back to Worland after my divorce. Thanks to a very good friend, I was introduced to Michele, fell almost immediately in love with her, and have been falling ever deeper in love with her ever since.

Upon getting married we moved to Denver. My father and I had closed our family business as he had been diagnosed with prostate cancer. I was rehired by my previous employer and had to report for work right after our honeymoon. Michele had graduated from a community college with an associate's degree in business, which she put to good use in her first job as a receptionist. Yes, I say this tongue-in-cheek; she eventually worked her way into a sales position with the same company and, ironically, she was selling business office furniture.

My employer was APS Inc., known more commonly as Big A Auto Parts. There was a long history between this company and my family; my mother and father met each other in one of the company stores; one of my father's best friends was a sales manager for the company and this gentleman and his wife served as godparents for my little brother. Regardless, I started at the bottom of the ladder with Big A and worked my way up the ladder a total of three times. Eventually I saved enough money and with the help of a dear friend bought and operated a Big A Auto Parts store in 1995. My dream became a living nightmare when the supplier, APS Inc., went bankrupt in 1999. Big A Auto Parts stores were then bought out by a competitor, which in itself is another story for another book.

CHAPTER 1

Our Life before Children

Michele and I had been married for ten years before we began our family. We were both immersed in our careers and professions. In August of 1990, Michele had finally been hired by United Airlines as a flight attendant, a childhood dream of hers come true. Her first domicile was Los Angeles; she commuted from Denver to L.A. during her on-duty days. I was working in sales with APS, traveling the states of Colorado, South Dakota, Wyoming and Nebraska. Our marriage was awesome; we enjoyed our time together since we spent so much time apart.

Our time together was spent sleeping in and dining out, shopping, and basically spending as much money as we earned. We had purchased our first home in 1988. It was a great first home. We built a huge redwood deck in our backyard. Michele loved to bathe in and get bronzed by the sun, and I enjoyed watching her.

During the non-snow months we played recreational slow-pitch softball at least one week night and during most weekends. Our friends were our teammates and we enjoyed spending as much time with these friends as we possibly could.

We also spent some of our time traveling back to Worland to visit Michele's parents. After my father passed away, my mother moved away from Worland to Cartersville, Georgia. This traveling gave us some very memorable quality time together as the drive was seven-plus hours; if you have ever driven from Denver, Colorado, to Worland, Wyoming, you understand the meaning of quality time. Michele would also accompany me during my customer calls when she could; this gave us the opportunity to spend more time together and for her to meet the people I was spending my time with. It also gave my customers the opportunity to get to know me and my family better. It was funny how showing up at an auto parts store with a very attractive female helped me sell more merchandise.

Looking back, I am very thankful for those times and look forward to the day when Michele and I can work and travel together again.

During the mid 80's to the early 90's, there was an acronym associated with married couples like Michele and I: "D.I.N.K.s" – dual income, no kids. We were the perfect example of D.I.N.K.s. No, we did not make a lot of money, but enough for us to pay our bills. Our savings amounted to a 401k plan that I had through my employer. As for Michele, she was working for United Airlines, one of the world's largest airlines, so she had a pension plan. Why we would put additional money into her 401k when she had a pension to look forward to?

As you can imagine, with Michele working for an airline company, we also took many opportunities to travel. I accompanied her on some of her flights while she was working as well. This was fun; she could wait on me at home, then I could catch a flight that she was working and she could wait on me and get paid for it.

Our most memorable trip was to Cancun, Mexico; it was like a second honeymoon, only better. Let me explain. On our wedding night, Michele and I drove to Casper, Wyoming, from Worland; we had a flight out of Denver the next morning, so this gave us a head start on the drive. Anyway, I had reserved a room at the Hilton Hotel in Casper and had ordered a bottle of champagne to celebrate. When we got to our room, I went to freshen up; Michele said she would open the champagne. The next thing I heard was a horrible scream; the cork had popped from the bottle and had hit her glasses. Though she did not have any glass in her eyes, she had a cut on one eye which of course swelled up and proceeded to turn black and blue. Picture the happy couple walking through the airport to their honeymoon destination – the groom and his bride with the black eye.

Cancun was magical though, no black eye, just white sand and turquoise, clear-blue water. The view from our room looked out onto the Gulf of Mexico and was as breath-taking as Michele was in her fluorescent-yellow two-piece bathing suit. One of our other trips was to Philadelphia, the city of brotherly love. I had never been there and wanted an authentic Philly cheese steak sandwich, so I took a redeye flight out of L.A. to Philadelphia with Michele. Now there's something that will get your attention: leave L.A. at 11pm, arrive in Philly at 5am, catch a short nap at the hotel, get up, go out in the freezing cold and rain, get the cheese steak sandwich, go back to the hotel, try and stay awake through the afternoon so you can sleep until morning, get up before the sun so you can catch a flight back to L.A., then home to Denver. All this from Friday night to Sunday morning, then back to work bright and early Monday morning. Those were the days.

I also took a flight from Denver to L.A. right before the start of Desert Storm, the first US military confrontation since Viet Nam. I wondered if I would get back home to Denver in order to be at work on Monday; then I wondered why the world appeared to look different. L.A. seemed smoky to me rather than the usual smog and fog. Michele and I also spent Christmas in L.A. one year; nothing says Christmas day like a trip to Disneyland, which reminded us of our honeymoon without the black eye. Yes, we spent part of our honeymoon with Mickey and Minnie Mouse; we were in our early 20's, remember, and from Wyoming, for crying out loud.

Another Christmas was in the nation's capital, Washington D.C. I remember walking from the hotel to a nearby mall. We went to see a movie, "My Life" with Michael Keaton. I bawled my eyes out. My father had passed away by this time so the movie was a reminder of how precious life is. When the movie was over we had to walk all the way back through the mall and to the hotel, tears running down my face, Michele holding my arm.

Yet another Christmas was spent in Vancouver, Canada. Michele was working the flight and her crew was so much fun; everyone had brought along food and beverages so we could all get together and celebrate when we arrived. Our flight landed close to midnight, Christmas Eve. At the hotel we partied like rock stars until early in the morning. Our flight out the next morning came too early. I remember sleeping as the crew was working the flight back to L.A., and how sorry I felt for them, because if they felt as bad as I did, they probably needed sleep too.

Drag racing was another form of entertainment we enjoyed; nothing says fun like sunny skies, the smell of rubber and nitro methane, cold beer and women wearing short shorts.

Before you think too badly of me here, stop. Michele was always surrounded by men when she was at home; my best friends were single and our home was their second home. Michele was young, attractive and fun to be with. Her personality was such that she made everyone she was with feel comfortable, welcome and cared for.

Thus was our life before children: care free, no real responsibilities except to one another. Our time was our time; no rushing around to doctors and therapists, no trips to the hospital in the middle of the night for a child with whooping cough or a split lip. No worries about the future and if we would have enough money saved for retirement, let alone enough to care for two boys that would not be able to earn and save for themselves.

"Perfect," as Michele called our relationship. Perfect, which, just like beauty, is in the eye of the beholder. She was right, though; looking back, it was perfect. In our eyes and in our lives, what we had was pure joy and love, in abundance.

CHAPTER 2

Starting Our Family

In the spring of 1994, Michele began talking louder about having children. She stated that we were in our tenth year of marriage, we both had good careers with good companies, we made decent money and that "we" should be "ready" to have a child. During our courtship and marriage, Michele had been on birth control pills. (Do not read anything into the fact that our sons have Down syndrome and Michele was on the pill; the mere thought is nonsense.) In the spring of '94 Michele and I finally agreed we had had enough practice; it was time to make a baby!

This reminds me of a story of when Michele and I were dating and I had already asked her parents for their blessing to marry her. I was helping Michele's dad put up a new fence around their spacious backyard – you know, winning favor with my soon-to-be father-in-law. The fence we were building was a three-rail post fence: round logs about eight inches in diameter and twenty feet long, and heavy. To attach the rail log to the fence post, pilot holes were drilled in the rail and the two spikes, which are more commonly known as twelve-inch long oversized nails, are driven through the pilot holes in the rails into the posts. Very shortly after I began hammering on these spikes, I began to tire and would miss hitting the spike, to which my soon-to-be father-in-law commented, "Sure hope you're a better lover than you are at driving those spikes, otherwise I'll never have grandkids by you."

If you are wondering, my father-in-law and I have a very good relationship, so much so that sometime near the time Michele and I decided to bring a child into the world, we were visiting Michele's parents, and her dad and I had the following conversation:

"So Kelly, what did you think of my daughter ten years ago when you married her?"

My reply, "I thought I'd like to love her brains out." (This is the "G" rated version.)

Her dad inquired, "What do you think of her now?"

I replied, "I think I've done a pretty good job."

When Michele had confirmed that she was indeed pregnant, she sent her parents a greeting card with the sentiment, "Looks like Kelly finally hit the nail on the head."

On a serious note; my father's last days on Earth were spent in the hospital in which Michele's mom, dad and older brother worked. They made my dad as comfortable as he could be, and Michele's dad, Marty, was with my dad when he passed away. I will never forget when Marty called and gave me the news and said he was flying to

Denver so he could escort us back to Worland to be with my mother and help with the funeral arrangements. Upon arriving, Marty hugged me and let me know that my dad had passed away very peacefully with a final gasp of air. I picture that gasp of air like the reaction you have to the gift you have always wanted, the happy gasp you take in as you see the gift and break out in the biggest smile you could possibly have. Marty also told me, "Son, I know that you and your dad were as close as any father and son could ever be, and I'm not your dad and won't ever be able to take his place, but if you ever need anything from me or even just someone to talk to, you can count on me." Thanks for this Marty; I'll never forget you and I'll always love you for saying this to me and for meaning it.

In July of 1994, or sometime very close – my memory is clear, it is the dates that are fuzzy – besides, no one knows I am writing this yet, so I cannot very well go to Michele and ask, "Honey, what day did you find out that you were pregnant?" She would want to know why I was asking, then I would have to tell her I am writing a book, and then she would probably have a whole lot of other questions that I am not prepared to answer just yet. So, in July of 1994, Michele took a home pregnancy test which indicated she was with child. She went to the doctor and confirmed the fact – she was pregnant.

My fatherly instincts kicked in: "I've got to stop traveling as much as I am so I can be here at home with my wife and child." So what did I do? I cashed in my 401k and spoke with my best friend about investing in an auto parts store. He would be a silent fifty percent owner and I would operate the store on a daily basis. If all went according to plan, the business would be paid for by 2002 and he and I could buy or open up another store and build an empire that would serve as a legacy for his family and mine.

With the business plan set and approved, we bought a store in Loveland, Colorado; a nice little business that needed some tender, loving care. With the proper attention and a lot of hard work, we knew we could accomplish what we had set out to do. It was at this same time that my new partner and best friend's wife happened to be in Denver to pay Michele and me a visit. It just so happened that Michele had a doctor's appointment during the time of her visit. As it was inventory time at the warehouse where I worked, I decided my best friend's wife could accompany my wife to her first ultrasound.

Being paged to the front lobby during inventory surprised me. Michele was waiting for me when I got there. I was happy to see her, but scared that something was wrong. She told me that she had a picture that was taken during her doctor's visit. It was a thermal image picture taken during the ultrasound and it had a caption written on it, "Hi Dad, we're twins!"

My mind went back to a conversation Michele and I had had during a walk we had taken a few evenings earlier. She had said that she was just barely pregnant but she was already having morning sickness, and that she did not like being pregnant. She said she hoped she could have twins so she could just be pregnant once, have her two kids and not ever have to be pregnant again. Of course I agreed, being the supportive husband and all.

I sat in a chair in the corner of the lobby. I could hear two voices in my head, one was saying, "Smile, dummy! Look at your wife and tell her how happy you are and that this just the best thing that could ever happen."

The other voice was saying, "Pick up the phone and call your mother. Not only are you going to be a father, but it is TWINS."

Suddenly longing for my childhood, you guessed it; I picked up the phone and called my mommy. "Twins," I said when she answered. "Can you believe it? I'm going to be the father of twins."

I was in shock, but after hearing the reassuring voice of my mother, I hung up, and being the smart dad, began performing damage control. "Sweetheart," I said, "your wish has come true. I'm so happy; how are you taking the news?" Michele, being herself, was not mad that I had had to call my mother; she in fact laughed at me, and then told me I would be taking her out to dinner that evening. In the meantime, the receptionist had made the announcement over the paging system to everyone in the building, "Your attention please! Everyone please congratulate Kelly and Michele Krei; they are going to be the parents of twins."

My only other memory of that day was upon returning to the stock room to resume taking inventory. All my coworkers congratulated me, and then one stopped long enough to say, "Hey Kelly, I hear your wife is having twins. Congratulations. Who's the father?" I needed the laugh to bring me back from the surreal to the real world. Twins! I had just convinced myself that Michele and I could afford to have one baby – now it was two! Two mouths to feed, two sets of clothes, two cribs and, oh my gosh, the diapers we would go through!

Suddenly my plans to become a business owner increased in significance – the quicker the better. Adding to my anxiety was the fact that Michele's doctor was concerned about her well being and her work as a flight attendant. He had requested that she take an immediate leave of absence due to medical reasons. Fortunately, United Airlines granted the leave. No way could they have a flight attendant carrying twins pushing a five-hundred pound cart on an aircraft flying through turbulence at thirty thousand feet while dealing with hostile passengers.

This leave gave Michele plenty of time to think and prepare. She immediately began on the nursery, hand-painting a mural on the nursery wall of the Winnie the Pooh characters. It was beautiful and one-of-a-kind. Next she joined a Mothers of Multiples group. This was her first experience with a support group. I could only imagine a room full of women, all pregnant with twins or even triplets, talking about how life was about to change for themselves and their husbands. We husbands should have a group too, "Fathers in way over their heads and too late to turn back now," but sadly the acronym for my fathers' group was not as snappy as "M.o.M.s".

Next, Michele realized that our starter home would in no way be big enough to accommodate twins, so she set out house hunting, and as luck would have it, she found one. A nice big, huge, beautiful brand-new home. "Honey, our children will be so much happier in this new home. Think of the room! As our children grow, this house is big enough, and it has a nice big backyard, and there is a new elementary school being built near by and . . ." on and on and on she went; how could I say no?

One week before I became the owner of an auto parts store in Loveland, Colorado, Michele and I sold our first home and purchased our new home in Broomfield, Colorado. Being young and senseless, and tight with our cash, having just bought a new home and a new business – and did I mention we are expecting twins – we decided to save the money we would spend hiring a moving company and move ourselves. Now, this is okay when you are moving from one apartment to another apartment or say from your last apartment to your first new home, but in hindsight, this was a lot of work and the tension it created was immense. Nevertheless, we did it, and on September 15, 1995, I became the owner of the Big A Auto Parts store in Loveland and commuted thirty-two miles one way each day, Monday through Saturday.

I have skipped many details of Michele's pregnancy, some out of respect for my wife and some because they have no relation to the purpose of this book. I would like to note that during the forty weeks of Michele's pregnancy we did not know and did not have any indicators or any suspicions that Kyle and Hunter would be born with Down syndrome.

Statistically, Michele did not fall into a risk category; therefore we did not seek to discover any "what ifs."

CHAPTER 3

Your Sons, Both of Them, Have Down Syndrome

March 11, 1995: I arrived home after work and per my normal routine, kissed Michele and headed for the fridge and an icy cold Coors Light. Michele announced she had been having contractions and they were happening more frequently. She had a bag packed and ready next to the front door. Next I heard, "Would you please call the hospital and let them know we are on our way?" Being me, I told her to relax and asked if her water had broken. I was a graduate of Lamas class and I had learned that until the water breaks, there is no emergency. Besides, the doctor had said that false labor pains would occur the closer she got to her due date.

I turned from the fridge to see Michele in the spare bathroom; the door was open. If it was physically possible, she would have been doubled over. "My water has broken. Get my bag and get the car out of the garage." She was not joking and I was not making light of her situation; I calmly informed her that I would now call the hospital as she had suggested moments earlier. Of course this was merely my attempt to buy time; after all, I had just cracked open an icy cold Coors Light and it would be such a shame to waste it.

Out of the bathroom and out the door to the garage she went. She was in the car waiting for me and did not speak, but I heard about this later, I assure you: "All you wanted to do was drink that beer while I was getting ready to deliver your children." There was a voice in my head and I could not determine whether the voice was high pitched or that of Linda Blair from the movie "The Exorcist". It was about 6pm and the evening rush hour was still in full blaze; it was also Friday night. So I determined the quickest route to the hospital would be to avoid the highway which could lead to delays, which could then lead to us being featured on the ten-o-clock news. I approached a red light just a few blocks from the house; this traffic light was not the first we had encountered, nor would it be the last on our way. Seeing that the light was red, I began to stop, but then the voice appeared again and this time I knew it was Linda Blair. I looked at Michele to see if her head was spinning around on her shoulders while she was demanding, "Run the light, run the light!"

We arrived safely at the hospital. I pulled up to the emergency doors and alerted the nurses that I had a crazy pregnant woman in my car and I would like to drop her off. I left short of asking them to call me when Michele had returned to normal as I was not sure if she had ever been in a normal state to begin with. When I had parked the car and entered the hospital with Michele's suitcase, I was escorted to a very sterile, cold, rather "blah" waiting room; I think the hospital called it a "staging area". It was not the room in which expectant mothers delivered; it was the room where the hospital personnel parked their patients and when delivery became certain, administered an epidural if so desired, then gleefully wheeled the patient to the "delivery room".

Our hospital of choice was in truth chosen by our doctor, since his practice was conducted in an adjoining office complex and he was highly respected within this particular hospital. I will say this: Dr. Stephen Volin, his staff and the staff of North Suburban hospital took excellent care of my wife and children during this entire ordeal. I will speak more of them later.

Michele and I had made a few decisions regarding delivery ahead of time: first, she would have an epidural (Michele does not like being in, nor do I like seeing her in, pain); and second, these boys (at this point it had been detected via ultrasound or sonogram that they were in fact male), these twins, would be our only children. We had had a previous conversation with the doctor; as soon as he delivered our sons, he would perform a "tubal ligation," thus tying her tubes to prevent future pregnancy. "Why tie her tubes?" you ask. During this time there was some evidence relating to a link between male vasectomies and the occurrence or frequency of prostrate cancer. My father's ultimate demise began as prostrate cancer; therefore we, Michele and I, had decided that she would have her tubes tied.

The pushing began at about 10pm and was one of the most brutal experiences of my life to that point. Poor Michele, not having ever delivered children before, was afraid to push like she had been instructed for fear of delivering more than just a child, thus placing her in an embarrassing situation with the doctor. Like lying on a table, naked from the top of her overwhelming belly down, legs spread, feet in stirrups, screaming bloody murder would be less embarrassing.

Finally, delivery! At 12:01 am twin A, Kyle, was delivered. Another instruction to the doctor was that the boys were to be born on the same day, and so prior to 12:05 am Saturday, March 11, twin B, Hunter, was brought into the world.

Silence. It was silent in the room. The doctor and nurses were silent, the boys were not crying, and there was a calm yet nervous manner between everyone in the room. One of the nurses explained that both boys were fine and in no danger; they were being cleaned and prepared for us to hold. This was taking place in a room connected to the delivery room with a window through which we could see doctor and nurses huddled together, taking care of our children; yet they were speaking so softly we could not hear them.

Earlier that evening, our friends had been playing softball and I had gotten word to them that we were at the hospital. After the game, the female friends brought me something to eat and before Michele went into hard labor, they separately got to go in and visit with Michele before her game began. Some stayed until the boys were delivered; they waited in, of course, the "waiting room".

The doctor reentered and immediately closed the door to the room we were in. The friends that were still there had gathered just outside, but the doctor had something to say that he wanted us to hear before our friends heard it. He had the nurses hand each of us a son, then he looked at both of us, in our eyes, and said, "Your sons, both of them, have Down syndrome."

It is hard to describe all the emotions that I went through at that very moment. I was excited about my sons entering this world but at the same time, I was scared at the news that had been delivered with them. In some way, I felt hollow; as if someone had kicked me in the chest so hard it had knocked the breath out of me. Too scared to be shocked, I was concerned for Michele; she had just delivered two children and was physically exhausted. Now she had just learned that her children had been born with a disability. My concern was for her well-being, both physically and emotionally. How would she deal with this? What could I do to make it all better?

Michele went into shock and rightfully so. She cried uncontrollably. I stayed with her until she slept and that came with the aid of a sedative administered by doctor's orders.

It was two in the morning. I had sent my mother home; she needed rest and I needed her rested so that she could be back at the hospital early in the morning in order to help me with whatever I might need help with. Not knowing anyone else I could call for help, I went to a payphone and called Michele's parents in Wyoming.

Not knowing what else to say, I informed Michele's father, Marty, that he was now the grandfather of two little boys and that his daughter was sleeping. Then I asked him what he could tell me about Down syndrome. I remember a pause, and then he calmly explained what he knew, medically, about Down syndrome. This was the second conversation with someone in the medical profession that had no "joy of childbirth" tone to it. All I really remember of the conversation is him telling me that barring any health-related concerns, the boys would be just fine and in time, we would learn more about the disability. So I made it my priority to make sure that my children were in no immediate medical danger. Then I focused on Michele and her state of mind.

As it was now after three in the morning, I realized I needed to get home, clean up and return to the hospital. I wanted to be with Michele when she woke up so that she would not be scared and alone. I checked in with the nursery and let them know that I would return in a few hours. The nurses informed me that one of the boys (I do not really remember which one) had a low blood oxygen level and was in an oxygen tent. The other was sleeping peacefully.

From the time I left the hospital until the time I walked into the grocery store to buy Michele some flowers at 7am, I do not remember anything. The only reason I remember the store was that our favorite clerk had given us a scrapbook as a gift and she wanted to know if Michele had delivered yet. For the first time I suddenly began to cry as I tried to explain what was going on. I am sure I did a horrible job of letting this very caring woman know that I was a proud father.

When I arrived at the hospital Michele was already awake, in pain and crying. She apologized to me and I immediately let her know that she was not to blame for the fact that our, let me repeat that, that OUR sons, had been born with Down syndrome. Next, I wanted to hold my sons, so I called the nurses' station and asked if that was possible. Michele said that she was not ready, so I went to the nursery and held each little boy and cried. I told each of them that I promised to take care of them and to love them. I would figure out this Down syndrome thing and I would be the best dad they could ever ask for. We would have a loving family and our lives, mine and Michele's, would be so much better because they, Kyle and Hunter, had been given to us as a gift.

Next I returned to Michele. She was not ready for visitors; and in fact when our friends heard the news, most stayed away. Those that did visit caused Michele to start crying again, so we kept most away unless they were on a list that was policed by the nurses and those at the visitors' desk. One visitor however, changed our lives in a magical way. She was the neonatal nurse from the delivery room. I think her name was Pauline; it is a shame I do not remember for sure. What I do remember is that she gave us some information that would help us to cope and to understand what Down syndrome (DS) was. She explained that she knew of an organization that supported parents of children with DS and that she would have someone call, with our permission. We agreed, and on Monday, March 13, another angel appeared in our lives.

This talk of angels may bother or make some uncomfortable, but until this very moment, and I am referring to the very moment I am typing these words, I never realized this: my father passed away on March 13, 1985 and we were about to meet someone that would change our lives in a very positive way on March 13, 1995.

Her name was Robin and she was a volunteer new parent visitor from Mile High Down Syndrome Association (MHDSA). She brought us a new parent package with information on Down syndrome and the organization she represented. She encouraged us to attend a parent support group meeting and told us about her family, including her son Tommy, who had Down syndrome. She was pleasant and easy to talk with and she gave us comfort; comfort in that she too had experienced the emotions we were going through. She reassured us that with care, love and support, we too could learn, adapt and face our new challenge.

Included with the package she presented to us was a book, *Babies with Down Syndrome: A New Parents Guide*, published by Woodbine House. This book was invaluable, not just for the information it contained but also for the meeting we were to have the next day with our new pediatrician. I read the book from cover to cover during the remainder of that Sunday so that I could be prepared with intelligent questions for the doctor. He was to arrive at Michele's hospital room about 10am, Monday morning.

Mind you, this was 1995. The worldwide web, aka "the internet" was still in its infancy; therefore finding information was not as easy then as it is today. As I think about it, today with all the information we have at our fingertips is as impressive as it is scary. Some of life's situations need to be taken on as a challenge rather than avoided as an inconvenience.

The doctor arrived as scheduled. We had been told in advance that he had experience with children with Down syndrome and we were very anxious to meet him. He was pleasant and did not treat the visit as a sterile event. After introducing ourselves I wasted no time in presenting my list of questions: "When will this test be done? Should we check for this symptom? What if Michele is unable to breastfeed? There is a murmur in one of the boys' hearts, when can we schedule an appointment with a specialist?" On and on I read my list and he listened without interrupting me. When I had finished, he calmly looked at me and explained that he was very aware of the boys' current conditions and that all my concerns would be addressed in due time. "However," he said, "right now it is important that you enjoy your babies and being new parents."

Once again I felt humbled by the circumstance and by his sense of calm. The good doctor had given me permission to celebrate the birth of my sons and being a new parent. He explained that Michele and the boys would be released from the hospital as soon as he and the nursing staff were comfortable that the boys were taking in the proper amount of mother's milk. At that time, we were to make an appointment to bring the boys to his office and from there we would establish a schedule for their necessary medical care.

What a relief! Finally someone who knew what the heck this Down syndrome thing was and how to respond to it!

In the meantime, we had to get Michele into the mode of mothering; her outlook was much like a rollercoaster, going from high to low from hour to hour. However, each hour she became more resolved that she would mother and love and care for her sons like she had planned on doing for the forty weeks prior to giving birth. Her first hurdle was breastfeeding. Due to low muscle tone, neither of the boys could suck hard enough to draw any milk, so plan B kicked in. We broke out the breast pump.

After an extra couple of days in the hospital getting the boys acclimated to this process, we were ready to go home.

CHAPTER 4

Babies Don't Come with Operator's Manuals

Stop laughing! Before leaving the hospital we had to watch a video that explained what to do in certain situations. For instance, we were instructed how to perform CPR on an infant in the event that one of the boys stopped breathing, and other such disasters. Then we were handed a list of things to watch for...you get the idea. We were scared out of our minds! Going home with a newborn can be traumatic, but going home with twins that have a disability is like diving off the high board and not knowing how to swim. Exciting, yes, but I would rather watch someone else do it first.

Our first decision as new parents was that we would sleep in shifts. This way the feedings and diaper changes could be handled by one of us while the other got some rest. To help us achieve this, during the day while the boys were taking a nap, Michele would pump her breasts for milk and store it in bags that were dated and placed in the freezer. Michele, being the organized person she is, would have a day's worth of bottles in the fridge so that we could monitor consumption. We also learned very early on to monitor what exited from the boys; blocked bowels are not a pretty picture, especially between the hours of midnight and 7am, or anytime during my shift.

By accident we established routines which would later become a saving grace. We made notes of lots of different things, both mentally and in writing, and we noticed what worked well and what did not. For example, we noticed very quickly that we had to wrap the boys up very tightly in their blankets in order to get them to settle down and go to sleep, and we also noticed that we had to get them each to sleep before we could lay them in their cribs. That is exactly what I am saying: if one did not sleep, neither slept, which in turn caused neither Michele nor I to sleep.

It was also funny to me how we discovered certain things that worked in different situations. For instance, one would eventually go to sleep while the other was awake due to a discomfort of some sort, so out of pure exhaustion, we would put the non-sleeper in a car seat and place the car seat in the doorway of our bedroom closet. When placed just so, the fussy one would suddenly grow sleepy and drift into the land of rest. We also had these motorized swings that would double as beds when the boys refused to sleep in their cribs. When the swings were carefully placed within arm's reach of the couch, the "on shift" parent was able to catch some much-needed rest as well.

CHAPTER 5

Changing Gears

It has become painfully obvious to me that I may be writing something that could be incredibly impactful on at least one life, if not many; yet I struggle with the details, as most of them are water under the bridge and, more often than not, sad. So as I sit and read through what I have written thus far, it has become more apparent to me that I am writing the wrong story. The story I should be telling is how the birth of our sons has changed the course of the lives of my wife and me, and how we would never be where we are today had they never been born, not to mention had they not been born with Down syndrome.

When I began writing, my entire thought process was on how the boys having Down syndrome has affected and changed our lives. However, the more I look at our lives (though I say "our lives" the boys do not know a life any different than the life they have), the more I see it is Michele and me that have gone through a tremendous change, and we continue to experience change. Now, as I realize that we have been through some of the toughest struggles of our lives, I see that it is how we have grown and become more that is the important story – the story my heart tells me to tell you.

All of the previously-mentioned information is true and accurate, especially that of our marriage prior to the birth of our sons. Our marriage was perfect, wonderful and care-free. The birth of our sons did not, I repeat, did not, ruin, destroy or wreck our marriage. As I look back up to this point I see we are responsible for everything that we have been through. In deeds, actions and thoughts, we are the ones that are responsible. There, I said it, and it did not hurt, not now anyway. Up to this point it hurt too much to say the words, but not now, which is the biggest reason that now seems the best time to put in written form our life and how Down syndrome has changed it.

You have read correctly, but let me write it again: our lives, our marriage, the relationship between Michele and I were all changed the moment Kyle and Hunter were born. Yes, these two sons of ours have Down syndrome and yes, we had many concerns when they were born, like: What does this mean for their health? Will they love us? How can we care for them? When can I hold my sons? Will they know that we love them without question? You might see that these would be questions any new parent might have; we were simply faced with an additional factor: Down syndrome.

As far as I could tell, Kyle and Hunter did not know or recognize that they were any different. They cried like babies do, they wore diapers, drank from a bottle, liked to sleep during the day so they could keep us up at night and all the other things that babies do. The difference was how people reacted to us and to our sons. I once said that a good way to find out who your true friends are is to be faced with a disability, because your true friends stick around. The others leave, noticeably and quickly; they disappear forever. So far, I can honestly say that I am better off with and because of my sons and nonetheless for those departed.

Do not get me wrong, we too took the news of our sons' disability very hard; Michele cried for days, then weeks, then months. Just when she felt she was ready to take her babies out into the world like new mothers do, she would be faced with stares and looks of disbelief. I also concede that our sons were not the best-looking babies, but today they are and continue to become the most handsome little boys.

In the early months of the boys' lives, it was Michele that persisted. She would venture out with the boys to the park, or to a restaurant, or to get their picture taken with the Easter bunny. Sometimes she would return home with great memories and sometimes with great tears, but to her credit, she kept taking the boys out. She would discover over time places to go that she felt comfortable going. Through the years, we continue to go to those places as we are welcomed when we go and the boys are met with smiles and understanding and the comfort that they are welcome too.

We were also fortunate that we were introduced to Mile High Down Syndrome Association. We have met some people that we would never have met if it were not for Down syndrome – people that have become and remain friends, people that have helped us as they have already been through some of what we are going through, and people that are new parents who we can help in turn by what we have been through and learned.

Probably the single smartest thing we ever did was to get the boys involved in therapy at a very early stage, six months old. We went to occupational therapy and physical therapy in the same way the parents with "normal" babies go to play groups. We were also fortunate that we were embraced by many individuals and organizations that realized that with twins we needed help, emotionally and financially. These folks also knew how to be there when we needed them and to give us our space when we needed space.

We also paid attention to not trying to reinvent the wheel. We read stories about and talked with parents who had traveled the road we were currently on, and we knew that the advances in medicine and society are due in large part to the efforts and experiences of these families. All we had to do was to continue to benefit from the past and learn and improve in the present so that the future might possibly be better.

As you might imagine, we also encountered many things we would never attempt. This too has provided us with insight into the minds and lives of others. Like many others, we wondered both to ourselves and aloud when our sons were born, had we done something to cause the boys to have Down syndrome? As time passed, we discovered more than just the fact that not only had we not done anything "wrong," but we had been given a gift, though it seemed to be wrapped in trouble. We had two wonderful gifts.

There is no "cure" for them as there is nothing "wrong" with them. They just seem to be a little slower, but in many ways, they understand much more about us, our thoughts, actions, behavior and love than we could imagine.

Maybe it is just me, but I was quick to try and fix something that first, could not be fixed and second, did not need fixing in the first place.

CHAPTER 6

Be Careful What You Wish For

Back to August, 1994: Michele and I were out for a walk after eating dinner one evening. It was hot out and Michele was beginning to feel miserable being pregnant. She did not like the sickness associated with pregnancy, nor the heat. As we were walking she said something that would later self-prophesize; she said she wished for twins so that she only had to be pregnant once, gain all the weight once, wear the "mommy-to-be" clothing once, be miserable once.

September 1994: her wish came true: twins. Imagine her shock and joy as her doctor handed her a picture of the sonogram that had just been performed and inserted in the picture were the words, "Hi, Mom, we're twins."

Thoughts of every kind entered her mind and mine. Thoughts like: two of everything – cribs, diapers, clothes, shoes, two mouths to feed and everything at the same time. There were also thoughts that brought great expectations: two sports stars, the first twin brother ticket to become president and vice president of the United States, twin prom kings and twin class valedictorians – the best of everything "twin".

Within a very short time, Michele's doctor requested that she stop flying until after giving birth. This request was due to the additional growth she would experience in carrying twins. Later in the pregnancy, she was required to limit her activity to three days a week and four days of rest; then towards the end, five days rest and two days activity.

So, very early in her pregnancy, she went about preparing the nursery. She borrowed an overhead projector from a friend to begin the mural on the wall of the boys' first bedroom. She hand-stenciled all the characters of Winnie the Pooh on one wall, then hand-painted each character. It was magnificent, but it also took a toll on her back, which is why I suppose the doctor recommended more days of rest than activity.

There would be no amniocentesis test; Michele was in her early thirties and did not fit the statistical characteristics of giving birth to children with disabilities. Nor was there ever any concern or signal that there was any problem with her pregnancy. Looking back, there was nothing wrong; everything was at it was supposed to be. She carried the boys into her fortieth week, which was good for twins; the boys were born just slightly premature. When she went into labor, she was cared for by the best doctor we could have ever hoped to have had, and he had plenty of staff to care for the boys once delivered. Every detail, every moment was just how it was supposed to be. The only element missing was the "joy" we were supposed to experience when the boys were born.

Beyond the initial shock, grief and disbelief came joy and tears of happiness and pride. The relationship that Michele and I shared would get us through this time in our lives; at least to a point where we could seek the help and support of others.

"Be careful what you wish for." It would take ten years from time the boys were born for us to truly understand this statement. We attract things into our lives by wishing. Call it what you want: the law of attraction, the power of thought; decisions and choices determine our lives. The most difficult decision we can ever face is how we choose to respond to the results of our wishes.

I have thought back more than once to my vow to Michele on our wedding day: to have and to hold, in sickness and health, for richer or poorer, in good times and bad, 'til death do us part. Our choice had been to have children and become a family. Fortunately for us our love for each other and for our sons would hold us together in the tough times ahead. We would learn in time that our sons' disability would lead us to a life and love we would never have known without them.

Based on how we were perceived by some, our wishes changed. When people would look at us with unbelieving faces, we would wish for acceptance; when others offered sympathy for our sons' disability, we would instead wish for encouragement; when we heard of others living a life that offered very little, we wished for more life for all and less to none; when faced with IQ tests that categorized our children as developmentally disabled, we asked for higher expectations and an educational environment that nurtured and promoted self worth in and for our children. We learned very quickly that our actions, deeds, thoughts and dreams would very quickly become our reality. We sometimes called ourselves "advocates" for our cause, when in reality we became "diplomats" for a community of human beings that deserve every opportunity, every high expectation and every right to a meaningful life.

Our choices and decisions took on a different meaning when we were making them for our children who literally could not speak for themselves. Some of our choices and decisions may have seemed very self-centered and biased, but were always made in the best interests of our children. We would learn in time to pick and choose our battles and sometimes decide to overly-protect our children. "Sacrifice" is a word that was often used in describing our lives; however, we reminded ourselves that we decided to have a family and that our wish was to sacrifice what we had for what could be. Our test is in how we respond to our wish.

Now mix in a marriage and all the complexities involved in building, maintaining and sustaining a relationship and you have the makings of very explosive powder keg.

CHAPTER 7

Counting Beans

In the early years of our lives as parents we learned, at considerable expense, the story of counting beans. Though you may have heard this story under another name, the moral of the story always remains the same, and that is to stop counting up everything you do and everything your spouse does not do and fighting about all the above.

If you would like a great way (and this is very sarcastic) to start or end your day, have an argument with your spouse about how he or she is not pitching in enough with the household chores. This will surely lead to even more constructive conversations like, "You need to earn more money," or my favorite, "Why do you come home from working hard all day long, play with the babies, eat your dinner and go to bed because you are tired and need some rest?"

As parents, we have multiple roles; all of them were at one time or another choices that each of us made. Choices like to fall in love, get married and work hard at our jobs or careers and to start a family and replicate the same through our children. Adding a special need of a child can complicate a relationship beyond belief. Or you can both, let me repeat that, both, make a conscious decision to recognize when you are not holding up your end of the deal and get busy making things right at home. Nothing, I repeat again, NOTHING, can wreak more havoc in your life than having an unhappy home life. It takes just as much work from man and woman, mother and father, husband and wife to work all day at a job or in the home and keep your spouse happy by doing little things. So stop counting beans and start communicating – communicating in a productive way, not yelling or not speaking at all – real, honest-to-goodness communication. For example: "Honey, I realize you have worked hard all day, but I would really appreciate it if you would empty the diaper dumpster before you watch Monday night football." Or maybe this, "Honey, you have worked hard all day tending to the needs of our baby, let me help you by fixing dinner for you when I get home from work."

Why is it that we, most all of us, work so hard at falling "in love," but work so very little at "staying in love." Trust me, I know of what I speak and preach, and for your added benefit, if you will read this book before you have any problems, your life will be so much better. If by chance you have already had or are now in a rough spot in your marriage, know that there is hope that you can repair your relationship. It will take time and effort, but if you really meant what you said when you placed that ring on your spouse's finger, then you will quit making excuses and get busy making up for lost time.

Answer this question (to yourself, not out loud; your answer may get you in trouble): describe, as a percentage, what you give of yourself and what you expect in return from your spouse in your marriage. If you immediately answer, "fifty-fifty," I beg you to reconsider. If all you are willing to give of yourself is fifty percent, then I seriously question that you would expect to receive, much less tolerate, the same in return. Everything we do or do not do every day matters; everything we say or do not say every day matters. The true test is: can you do this every day? It is not enough to want to do, or try to do. Life can sometimes be very tough, but you have someone on this earth that thought enough of you to fall in love with you, and you thought enough of each other to have a child or maybe more than one. So why on Earth would you treat someone that you care for so much like the diaper dumpster? Instead, get your crap straight and take good care of each other. Notice all the way through here I ask that you take good care of "each other". When things are toughest it is easy to place blame on one person or the other, but the true test of a relationship and the character of each person in that relationship is their ability to make things better by being better themselves.

I constantly remind myself that I must work as hard now at staying "in" Michele's pants as I did twenty-four years ago when I was working to get in her pants in the first place. If I have not been clear on this up until now – I love Michele, she is my best friend, a beautiful caring woman, mother of my beautiful sons; I would die for her. So it goes without saying that it would kill me to treat her in a manner with any less love and respect than she is due. She earned this the moment she told me, "I love you."

I will speak more of a seminar that Michele and I attended later in this book: the seminar, "Love and Respect" presented by Dr. Emerson E. Eggerichs. The seminar came at a point in our relationship that found us both sick and tired of being sick and tired of each other. To say it saved our marriage would be fabricating the truth; we learned things about each other that we already knew. We also learned that if we kept making excuses and ignoring what we already knew, we would continue down our destructive path and would probably quit on each other.

Please, stop counting beans! If you insist, try counting different beans; see how many good things you can do without having to be patted on the back for doing them. In the end you either win or you lose. There is so much at stake – winning takes time, hard work, effort, laughter and tears, but the reward will last you a lifetime. Losing is much easier; all you have to do is quit.

CHAPTER 8

Establish and Cherish Routine

Call it boring, mundane, dull, dreary or monotonous, but without established routines, our children might drive us crazy and in turn, we would be adding unnecessary frustration to their lives. We found out very early on, and I am talking within the first six weeks, that if we did certain things in a certain way day in and day out, our children seemed to thrive on the certainty.

It may seem too simple, but picture if you will, we walk to elementary school every morning on the right hand side of the street. Coming home in the afternoon, if we followed the same path, we would be on the right hand side of street. However, if we were to follow our footsteps, coming home we would be walking on the left hand side of the street which is exactly what we did. Every day, for five years, first through fifth grades, we walked on the same side of the street, at the same time every morning, and we followed our footsteps home every afternoon, every school day.

Sound silly? Try and reason with a child that understands you but cannot communicate back to you all the thoughts that are racing through his or her mind. Rather than suffer a meltdown, either yours or your child's, bend a little (remember, pick your battles), and let your child have some routine. As an adult (before children) I fought routine as if it threatened my life; now that I am a parent of two children that have special needs, I have convinced myself that I will cherish routine as much as I value oxygen.

During the school year, you might just be able to set a clock by our schedule. We wake up between 6 and 6:30 in the morning; the boys are usually awake by this time too. We make coffee and feed the dogs, then I fix pancakes for Kyle and toast for Hunter. Each of the boys also has one link of sausage. I make the pancakes fresh each morning from a box mix, not frozen and heated in the microwave. Hunter likes cinnamon sugar on his toast. For dinner each evening, we have a meat, pasta and fruit. The boys drink milk with their dinner; in the morning they have either milk or juice.

Still think routine is boring? Our sons do not drink soda pop nor do they eat candy of any kind; both of these things are treats, and occasional treats at that. At most the boys have three to four cans of soda per month. Another definition of routine is "habit". Now I am not implying in any way, shape or form that our children do not eat their fair share of chips and popcorn, but we limit their sugar intake for their benefit as well as ours.

This is more habit than routine, but television is another distraction that our children are not addicted to. Yes, they each have a television in their room, but it is not hooked up to cable or local television. They watch videos or play video games, and their video game library does not contain any games in which blood can be seen spurting from any body part. There are no guns, knives or warfare. Any Disney movie is the movie of choice for Kyle and Hunter.

We have also seen that routine can highlight or bring out tendencies or traits such as obsessive-compulsive, also known as OCD. We have noticed that when the boys are involved in a routine activity, everything must be aligned just so and they must be happy with how things are arranged before proceeding. This in itself can and has caused frustration from time to time, but we continue to remind ourselves that our patience is being tested during the frustrating moments and that we just need to slow down so that the situation works itself out just as the boys like it to be.

Once again, we find ourselves being taught a lesson; that we take life in such a hurry rather than enjoying each moment, or living in the now rather than being in such a rush to get to the next step. Sometimes we do not recognize this due to our level of frustration, and let me tell you, the guilt and embarrassment make us stop and wonder, "What in the heck are we in such a hurry for?" It is only during school days when the bus is waiting that we really find ourselves stressed, but as our bus driver reminds us, "the bus isn't leaving without Kyle and Hunter."

Over the years we have adjusted our routines to fit the needs of our children and to in some way salvage our sanity. One thing remains constant: things change.

CHAPTER 9

Finding Purpose

The questions began the moment the boys were born: What does their birth mean? What purpose do I need to fulfill in my life or in theirs? What message am I supposed to be receiving from their birth? Am I supposed to be changing my life as a result of their birth? Question after question, all seemingly with no answer; at least I wasn't getting any. This is where the story really begins, at least for Michele and me. More for me than her, actually; she just happened to be caught in the middle. Fortunately for me, she rode out the storm.

I began by questioning my faith, which as you may remember was fragile at best since the death of my father. I asked God every day, "What are You trying to get me to understand or do?" "Why have You given me Kyle and Hunter and what lesson am I supposed to learn?" These questions and a million different variations went through my mind on a daily basis until one day I thought I had figured out where to start.

Working for the same employer for fourteen years, I had enrolled in a 401K, saved a decent amount of money and between myself and a lifelong friend had bought an auto parts store. My friend was a silent partner, so I was owner and operator. This began in September, 1995 and lasted until the supplier company that provided our parts went bankrupt, September 11th, 1998. The same company was taken over or bought out by a competitor, and by the end of 1999 our store had been consumed by the competitor. It was an ugly, nasty and vile transaction. I was told by those that I had worked with and for, "Don't worry, Kelly, we'll get you out whole. You won't get any blue sky, but you'll get out whole." Very soon I would find myself in a hole rather than "out whole"; the competitor decided that they did not like my building as much as they liked the one they already had. This left me with a lease on a building without a business to provide income. I also had just finished remodeling the building and had increased my stocking inventory by $100,000. I had taken out a second mortgage on my home to fund the remodel and the increased inventory was secured by a note with the bankrupt supplier, which was now in the hands of the competitor, and they were calling the note due. The timing was awful: just over three years into a seven year loan with the Small Business Association. I was barely making ends meet let alone able to write a check for $100,000.

My back to the wall and in fear of losing our home, Michele and I filed for bankruptcy in August, 1999. We managed to save our home and two of our three cars. The third car, which I had just taken out a loan to buy, I drove back to the dealership and walked six miles home in shame on a bitterly cold December morning. Another humiliation was having to include my friend in the bankruptcy. The competitor would not pay him the money he had invested in the business, nor would they pay my investment; my 401K, fourteen years of hard work, was down the drain. Ultimately the only debt the competitor bought was debt held by a lien holder and the note to the bankrupt supplier. The people I had worked with and for were now working for the competitor; they told me to "be happy with the offer you are getting and sign the paperwork before our new employer changes their minds and lessens the offer."

Bitter does not begin to describe my feelings, and to top it off, I now had to find a job. The competitor offered me a job which on the surface was acceptable, but within six months, the honeymoon was over and I was treated like all the other employees that had come over from the old company: "Take it and like it or hit the road" – which is exactly what I did. During the next five years I would work for five different companies, and in September, 2004, I made a decision that would send my life into an out-of-control spin that would financially destroy my family and nearly doom my marriage.

The decision I made in September, 2004 was to try my hand at network marketing. I was going to be a "home-based business owner" and make millions by helping others make millions themselves. Please do not misunderstand me or read anything into my remarks about network marketing; there are some outstanding companies with tremendous products, services and business opportunities. I, however, found that this business, network marketing, was not a good fit for me.

My decision to leave the security of my job and a steady paycheck was based on one simple statement from my supervisor at that time. I was summoned to his office and was told, in no uncertain terms, "You are placing a higher priority on your family than you are this company. You better take a look at where your pay comes from and get your priorities straight." In a matter of minutes I calmly walked to my car, gathered my sales binder and my company-issued laptop, returned to my supervisor's office, and quit right there on the spot. "Are you sure?" asked the supervisor.

"My family is first and foremost now and for the rest of my life," I replied. "I suggest you take as much interest in the people working with and for you as you do in the company that you work for. You might just find that the people working with and for you feel the same."

It took me two weeks to tell Michele that I had quit. I had received pay for accrued sick and vacation time, but when the time came to tell her I had quit my job and would not be providing a regular paycheck, the tension in our home and marriage began to build. For the next two years, I would try and fail miserably in my home-based business. During the years of 2005 and 2006 I earned a grand total of $6000.00. I had used up what little savings we had, maxed out all of our credit cards, and borrowed enough money from my mother to ruin her financially as well. Michele had taken a second job to help with expenses, but what we really needed was for me to start earning some money.

Along the way and partially due to what was happening to Michele and I financially, my mother moved in with us. She and her husband had had a conversation similar to the one I had had in 2004 with my supervisor; she too chose to place her heart and her priorities where they were needed most. This added additional stress to our already overloaded stress-filled life, but without my mother's help, Michele and I would no longer be married.

Finding purpose had become more than a priority. My life as I knew it depended on me finding purpose, making sense of everything in the past and getting my life going in a better direction. It started at a meeting that I was attending as part of my home-based business training. One of the components of any good network marketing company is training and personal development and had I not been involved, I most surely would not be writing this book. I should note that I had started with this particular company in May, 2001. It had been presented to me as part-time income and I could have used the service at the time I was losing my auto parts store; how ironic is irony anyway?

Details of the meeting and topic have escaped me; however, the message in that meeting was still very vivid in my memory and it was not until I had quit my job that the memory of what the speaker had said at this meeting would be forever burned into my everyday thought. The statement was this, "I appreciate all of you for attending tonight's training; however, I have only come here to speak to one or two of you…"

I have many notes of the rest of the meeting, but to this day, this statement speaks to me every day, and every day I answer back (in my mind or sometimes aloud), "Thank you, I'm the one you were sent to speak too."

"Purpose should drive and motivate you, but when life gets a little tough will you have the resolve to continue in your pursuit of finding and fulfilling your purpose?" It was at this point I began to sincerely and earnestly seek my purpose in life, and it was at this point that I would answer my fears with faith. I would resolve to seek truth and real answers to my questions, but rather than look for my answers to appear from a burning bush, I would know that my questions were being answered if I would simply pay attention and receive what I was asking for.

Someone that I respect and admire greatly told me, "If it is important and if it will change people's lives, you must ask yourself if you are willing to commit yourself to your purpose."

My purpose has also become multifaceted and revolves around my sons. The first thing I had to figure out was "what?" then "why?" For a long time I was stuck on "how?" but I was listening to a CD one day by Earl Nightingale titled "The Strangest Secret" and what he said struck me right between the eyes. He said, "All you have to do is know where you're going; don't concern yourself too much with how you are going to get there." Right then and there I knew I had heard this for a reason, and right then and there I started filling my mind with "what" I wanted to accomplish and decided to let the details of "how" take care of themselves.

Have you ever met or known someone that is so busy planning and going over every possible detail that absolutely nothing gets accomplished? Me too, and I have also heard that a confused mind does nothing. So I developed a very clear picture in my mind of what I wanted to accomplish, then I set about getting on with life. Part of the "how" is unfolding as I write this book or memoir and yet another part of the "how" is in your reading it.

CHAPTER 10

Lessons Learned

In addition to those listed in some of the previous chapters, some of the lessons I have learned in life would not consume more than a paragraph or more; therefore, I submit them here:

A Time to Grieve: First and foremost – new parents that have just received a diagnosis or are parents of a newborn with Down syndrome or any other birth defect, please allow yourselves a time to grieve. It was hard for me to understand this for the longest time. After all, a new human life has been born; yet the baby, or in our case, babies, that we did receive came with some unexpected challenges. Our tears for the most part come from not understanding the gift we had been given, and our tears are for the loss of a dream. This being said, it is also okay for others to offer sympathy. A natural reaction to your sorrow experienced by family and friends is for them to express sympathy.

October 10, 2008: it has been one year to the day that I began this memoir; it has allowed me a tremendous outlet for grieving and reflection. It has also given me the opportunity to grow and become a better person, husband, father and friend. During this year I have asked myself, "What do I want to be remembered for?" and "What do I want to accomplish that will last long after I am gone?"

Faith or Fear: Notice I wrote "or" not "and"; the two cannot live together, not even for a second. Combining the two is like mixing oil and water, no matter how hard you try and how hard you shake it, the two do not mix. For every situation or circumstance we find ourselves in, we must either have faith that we can survive it, or fear that we will not. When my sons were born, I questioned my faith, and for many years, I denied my faith until I finally realized that my faith was so strong that it would not be denied.

Yes, in life there are moments, times, situations and circumstances that cause us to question "Why?" Those with faith ask, "What is it that I am supposed to learn and how can I make the most of this situation?" Those that live in fear do not ask, or they make excuses and worse, place blame on others and life for their circumstance.

I know this; I do not know that as I grow older that my faith strengthens, but I do know that as I get older, my belief in my faith grows.

Responsibility: "I am responsible for my thoughts, decisions and actions (or inactions)." My Creator gave me the ability to make decisions and though all of my decisions may not be good ones, my Creator also gave me the ability to make bad decisions right. In what was the worst time of my life just two years ago, I looked at myself in the mirror and said, "What are you doing to yourself and your family? What are you going to do to fix it?"

Casting blame and finding excuses caused me to lose two years of my life and also nearly ended my marriage, which would have resulted in our becoming a statistic – marriages ending in divorce when faced with children that have a disability. It would take two more years to correct the damage of the prior two, but the next two years would be so much more enjoyable than the previous.

Wedding Vows: "Kelly, will you take Michele to be your wife? *Will you love and respect her*? Will you honor her? Will you stand by her in good times and bad?" I remember taking those vows June 16th, 1984, answering "I will". Somehow, twenty years later, I lost focus on the single most important person in my life, my friend and wife, Michele.

To her credit, she never gave up on me. She pushed me every day to be the person she knew I truly was. She was true to her vows; she stood by me in good times and bad. In my deepest darkest moments, it would finally occur to me that there were people in my life that believed in me more than I could believe in myself. It would also occur to me that the meaning of love goes way beyond just saying "I love you" and that love is more than just a feeling. In jeopardizing our home and finances, I had risked the trust of "love" that Michele had in me; then she gave me a card that I will cherish forever and will share with you here:

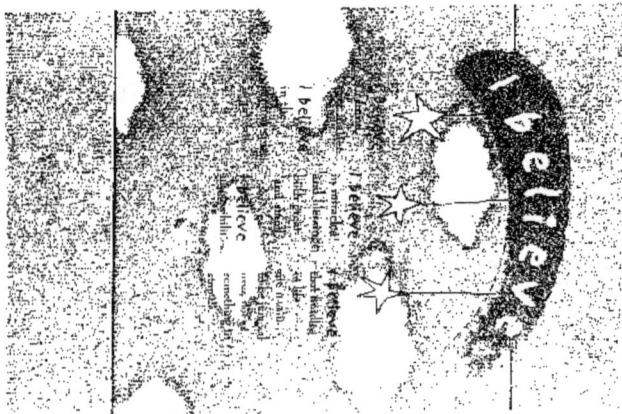

Life can present us with some difficult struggles and challenges, but when I said, "I will," I meant it, and so did Michele. She believed so strongly and confidently in me when I could not believe in myself; this, ladies and gentlemen, is the true meaning of love.

Our love and respect for each other, our children, our family and our lives has been our saving grace. Yes, it is true, we have at times said mean, hateful things to each other, but when calmer, cooler and more sensible heads prevailed, we knew then like we know now that we have a love for each other that cannot be replaced. This love and sincere appreciation that I have for Michele motivates, drives and inspires me every day to be worthy of her love and respect.

Have a Plan: I had never been big on goal-setting, to do lists or any variation of the sort until one day I heard someone say, "If you want to accomplish extraordinary things, you must plan extraordinary things to do." This hit me right between the eyes and since then, even though everything I want to accomplish may not be extraordinary, everything I want to accomplish gets written down. To my amazement, everything that I write down to do gets done, even without too much and sometimes absolutely no detail in my plans; merely writing it down brings it to fruition.

Very soon in this book I will share with you my goal for the developmentally disabled community and how I hope you will help.

Ask: Ask, and it shall be given you; Seek, and you shall find; Knock, and the door shall be opened for you. We have all heard, "Be careful what you ask for, you might just get it." I am here to testify that this works both well and not so well. I have also heard that opportunity knocks once; however, I do not believe this. I do believe that if we miss an opportunity it becomes someone else's and another bigger and better opportunity will present itself to us. I also believe that there are infinite opportunities in this life and that we ought to stop limiting our belief in just one, but rather, how many opportunities can we grasp?

Act: Do something, take action, proceed, work, accomplish, get busy; these are just a few of the definitions of "act". Without act, there is no action. Take a dream and no action and you will get NOTHING, except wasted dreams. "Build, work, dream, create" – words my father told me, but more than words; life without action is a failure of boundless potential. My father also told me to not let the label of "lots of potential" stick to me very long, for if I should, I might never get from underneath the weight of it.

I have also learned that there is a definite difference between being busy and being productive; some things we know and ignore until we get honest with ourselves and face reality. If you have several projects or tasks going on at the same time and nothing is getting accomplished, then it is time to pick one thing and get that one thing done.

For the previous two years I had let the condition of my lawn and home fall to the state of shame and disgrace; quite simply, our home was an eyesore. The front lawn needed to be replaced and the house needed painting and I was not about to do either myself. In my younger days, I used some of my vacation time to do these types of things and I also did them myself to save money. Now I needed to work to earn money in order to hire someone that would do these things for me. So, in January of 2008, I sat down and made a list of things that needed to be done; then I pri-oritized my list. I carried this list with me every day and when I was at the office I put the list on the keyboard of my desktop computer, this way it was in front of me at all times. I found that if I had to look at this list constantly, I would rather be looking at my accomplishments than a list of unfulfilled dreams.

> **Dream**: Big or small, we should all have dreams, stuff we would like to do, places we would like to go, books we would like to read, movies to see, food to eat, clothes to wear, cars to drive and homes to live in. Whatever you want, dream it, write it down, commit it to your thoughts so that you can visit your dreams often.

I have said this before and will say it again: none of us can foresee the future and as much as we plan, plans change. Life changes, sometimes almost instantly at times, and other times it becomes what it is due to the things we think and do day in and day out. If we could only condition ourselves to think very clearly about what our ideal future would look like while being grateful for all the good things we have now, we would all live better lives.

This leads me to a chapter that I look forward to writing but at the same time causes me a bit of anxiety; you see I have been called (by people that care for and love me) a procrastinator, but in my procrastination I have found some salvation.

CHAPTER 11

Everything Will Be Just Fine

I am known as many things by my loving wife, one of which is procrastinator. I resemble this remark in many ways, all of them good. A long time ago I heard that ninety-eight percent of the things we worry about in life never happen; thus my eagerness to wait and see.

Seriously though, when calmer heads prevail, better decisions can be made. If and when we find ourselves "reacting" to something, shouldn't we ask ourselves, "What is the best way to handle this situation?"

When Kyle and Hunter were born, I sought information on Down syndrome and what it meant to my children. When I learned that the condition was not life-threatening, I then turned my attention to support and what kinds of "help" were available. I also paid close attention to the wellbeing of Michele; her mental and emotional states were both fragile. As soon as she got past the initial shock, her motherly instincts kicked in. Yes, thirteen years later, she still cries from time to time and so do I, but we have learned to share our emotions and lives together and in doing so everything turns out just fine.

In the beginning of our children's lives we were introduced to therapy: occupational and physical. After a few years we mixed in some additional therapies: speech, music, art, warm water and horseback riding. Some had great impact, others not so much. The biggest lesson we learned was never to underestimate what the boys could do by letting ourselves or anyone else tell us what they could not do.

Elementary school was a big step for us and the boys. We had moved from our home in Broomfield for several reasons, all of them to do with our children. We wanted our children to be in Adams 12 school district; we felt at the time that Adams 12 had significantly better programs for the developmentally disabled. (Now, halfway through eighth grade, we still feel just as strongly.)

During the boy's elementary school years, we discovered that they behaved better if they were not together in the same classroom. (Yes, they attend public school and they attend regular classes with all the other neighborhood children – what a novel concept!) As they transitioned into middle school, we found ourselves having to put the boys in the same classroom setting for a portion of the day due to space and school budget limitations. In spite of it all, the boys and their teachers figured out a way to make this work; isn't that amazing! We worry about our children because we care, and we find that we are blessed with teachers, classmates and neighbors that care just as much as we do.

(I am no longer going to procrastinate; I am going to start worrying about high school right now. Eleven months will come and go before I know it, so let the worries begin!)

Once again, I find myself learning a lesson, but the lesson has nothing to do with my children having Down syndrome. Let me put it this way: in a few short days, Americans will vote on a number of things, a new president and hopefully for the first time, a female as vice president of the United States. We will also find ourselves voting on issues closer to home, like ending wait lists for the disabled – wait lists that are so long a person could find themselves being on the list all their life and never receiving the services for which they wait. I have even heard a great excuse not to vote to end the wait list: have the disabled write to their congressperson instead of raising our taxes to improve the dismal services that currently exist. Please!

Then there is this excuse: Down syndrome is not that bad, these people live fairly normal lives. Do they really need "services" in order to lead better lives? My response to this is simple and blunt, "My children were born with a developmental disability and make no excuses; what is yours?" The reasoning that individuals with Down syndrome having relatively normal lives is no excuse for excusing them from services or life or any other opportunity available to them. The fact is that the developmentally disabled community needs and deserves better than what it gets and I will spend the rest of my life fulfilling this mission.

Let me step off my soapbox and get back to "everything will be just fine for a moment." Whenever we have had to deal with a situation, be it an individual education plan (IEP), IQ test (you figure out what IQ stands for) or anything else imaginable that includes our children, we sit down face-to-face with the other party involved and figure out the best way possible to deal with it. Example: I received a notice from the school principal one day stating that the school was in "lockdown" due to an "unsubstantiated threat". Being me, I called the school and scheduled a meeting (face-to-face) with the principal. Having had similar meetings during my childhood, I knew just what I was in for. I wanted to know from the principal and from my children's teacher and care provider what plan was in place for my sons in the event that the school ever found itself in a "substantiated threat". The principal and my sons' teacher rolled out their plan and it was amazing that they had thought of every possible worst-case scenario and were prepared in advance.

Once again, I am reminded that "communication" can resolve so much more than a lack of it. I am also reminded that other people have the same concerns, worries, cares, problems, situations and life events that I have, and as long as I treat others the way they treat me, everything will be just fine.

I have also entered a new career or profession. November 1, 2006, I became a licensed insurance agent/producer in the state of Colorado, able to offer home and auto insurance to residents in my great state. I was very fortunate to meet a gentleman that took an interest in me, my family and my story. He owns the agency at which

I work and he and the fellow company owners of Affordable American Insurance offered me an opportunity to not only provide an income, but also an opportunity to give back to my community, specifically the developmentally disabled community.

In January of 2008, I was nominated for a community service award by the owner of the agency in which I work, with one of the insurance carriers we represent. I was awarded $15,000 for the organization I supported, Mile High Down Syndrome Association. In thirteen years, no one had paid a bigger compliment to my wife and me in honor of our sons. I was recognized by the CEO of Affordable American Insurance (AAI) during the corporate meeting and held a press conference with the local paper and city council representative. During these events, the CEO of AAI made a point of letting me know that I was a valuable and significant member of the AAI team.

I am fortunate to have found an opportunity with AAI. I produce a fair amount of insurance business for my agency and company, but the blessing that I have received as a member of this company far outweighs the income I am able to earn as a result of my policy production. I am recognized for my worth as a person, a father and a community member in addition to my contribution to the bottom line. This is something I have been looking for over the last thirteen years, an opportunity to make a living and make a difference.

My sincere and deepest gratitude goes to Barrett Bartels, the owner of the agency I work with and Tony (CEO) and Lissa Fernandez of Affordable American

Insurance. I am both proud and humble to work in a profession that enables me to provide products and services that give value to my clients, from the best of the best in the insurance industry by a leader in the independent insurance business, Affordable American Insurance.

CHAPTER 12

The Blind Dog Wins

Our family home consists of me, my wife, Michele; our sons, Kyle and Hunter; my mother, Emily; and our two dogs, Peanut Butter and Kookie. We have had P Nut for three years. We adopted her from a Sheltie rescue after our previous sheltie, Fraser, had to be put to sleep due to a tumor. P Nut has seizures that are somewhat controlled by medication but it is the most frightful experience to witness. Fortunately she only has them every five weeks and they usually last for an hour. Unfortunately most of the time she has them in the early morning hours between 1 and 3am. Other than this, P Nut is a faithful, loving friend and is exceptionally good with Kyle and Hunter.

Kookie is another story. Michele was introduced to Kookie when she was at the vet with Peanut Butter. Kookie had just been rescued from a chicken coop in Nebraska and Michele just happened to spot her while she was at the vet. Kookie was born without eyes and was estimated to be three months old. Michele immediately fell in love and called me to explain that she knew what she wanted for her birthday, Kookie. My immediate reaction was, NO, not another dog. After thinking about the tone of Michele's voice when she called, however, I called her back and told her that I was good with another dog.

People's first reaction to Kookie is, "How does that dog see?" to which we reply, "Not having eyes, she doesn't."

"How does she get around your house?"

Our reply, "Very well". Kookie is a Sheltie mix, the breed of the father is not known but if I had to guess, and I do, I would guess Pomeranian. She has beautiful golden hair and the fluffiest tail. She has a love for life and adventure that amazes me every day. She runs circles around our backyard with reckless abandon, she uses a doggy door to go in and out of the house and she never sits around feeling sorry for herself – she does not know any better.

Our sons, Kyle and Hunter, do not know to feel sorry for themselves either; since birth they wake up each day with Down syndrome and each night, they go to bed with Down syndrome – not special, not better or worse, just different. Yes, when we speak of our sons, we describe them as having "special needs," but Kyle and Hunter are not special, just different. Not long ago I was speaking with a gentleman that is a father to a young woman born with Prader Willi syndrome. He made a comment I will never forget, "We need these people; they make us better people because of themselves." How insightful and how tremendously accurate! Our children make us better because of the changes we make in ourselves due to the disability they were born with.

Back to Kookie; I was talking to Michele last night about how I continue to be amazed at how Kookie runs the yard, then she runs the house. Her senses are so keen. Michele responded, "She definitely makes the most of every day" and instantly I thought,

"She GETS the most out of every day"; literally, she gives every day everything she has and she gets everything she wants out of every day. The blind dog wins.

Now how, you ask, does this have anything to do with kids and marriages and relationships? Well, it has everything to do with everything in life. Look, if a blind dog can love and trust us without ever seeing us; this is a life well-lived. When our sons were born, we were not expecting them to be born with Down syndrome and for nearly fourteen years, we have found our way – through the therapies, the insurance claims, the school system, the hospitals, the doctors' offices, community center boards, support groups, daycare, no money and lots of bills, Staph infection, pneumonia, hysterectomy – for better and unfortunately worse and back to better again. We have bumped into our share of "life" much like Kookie bumps into a wall or door, but we gather ourselves together, we love each other and we move on. We fix our wrong decisions, we learn from the past and we grow from it, because like Kookie, though we may have to do it in the dark, we will find our way.

CHAPTER 13

The Trail

Do not go where the path may lead, go instead where there is no path and leave a trail (**Ralph Waldo Emerson**).

Currently, November 12, 2008, in the great state of Colorado there are approximately twelve thousand people with developmental disabilities on the state "wait list" for services. The types of services vary from housing to job training, and the services are dependent on the needs of the individual. Current estimates show that people on the existing "wait list" could live their entire adult lives "waiting".

Recently, during a conversation with a friend, I was asked a question that has haunted me since the day my sons were born, "What does the future hold for your children?" Here is what I do know about the future and my children: advances in medicine and science along with early intervention, i.e. therapies, and an evolving society tell us that people with Down syndrome will live into their mid-to-late 60's. Twenty years ago the life expectancy for a person with Down syndrome was 40 years. Knowing this and having the expectation that our children will live long lives requires our attention and a sense of urgency.

Across our state and nation, there are a multitude of agencies, organizations and families that are performing, operating and developing "services" that address the needs of the developmentally disabled and their families – some better than others, but all progressing and becoming better as time goes by. These various entities also provide niche services, programs and the like; each also have similar mission and vision statements and fight profoundly for donations and working capital. Some start in the family kitchen as a parent support group and grow into huge associations. With this growth comes the need for office space, buildings, leases, staff, payroll and board directors, all of which take more time and money.

Which brings me to the here and now: in my search for purpose and in looking for how I can make a difference in the lives of my children, the developmentally disabled community and the world, an idea was born. I have presented my idea to a few close friends and colleagues which has, in turn, resulted in my writing this essay, or memoir, or wish list. So here is my idea, which I am calling for now; "The Trail":

MISSION & VISION FOR "THE TRAIL"

An environment for the developmentally disabled and their families where all can feel welcome and comfortable and share an ordinary place within the community.

To provide the opportunity to develop a variety of relationships with an increasing number of persons

To offer the ability to exercise personal decision making in both large and small matters

To provide an opportunity to perform and engage in meaningful activities

To offer an appreciated place among a network of people and a respected role in community life

Maybe you will be able to relate to our daily lives and schedules, maybe not; but if not, you might empathize or understand, so play along. When our sons were still young enough to be in car seats, packing them up to go to therapy, or anyplace for that matter, was a major undertaking. I remember very well having a nice big SUV and needing all the storage space for diaper bags, strollers, extra clothes, coolers with juice, etc; then as we arrived at our destination, unloading all this stuff then reloading it again so that we could go to the next destination. I recall it was a tremendous amount of work and effort, and was, more times than not, frustrating.

But imagine, if you will, a place that has everything on the same campus or within the same complex: therapy, medical offices, various organizations, an activity center for young and old, a coffee shop for meeting, a library for quiet, a place to work out or just have fun, a nutritional center where you can find good food and gain knowledge, a movie theatre, a bowling alley and finally but most important of all, a place for the developmentally disabled to work and truly find a "sense of community" in an environment built around their community. This "place," "The Trail," would be for the developmentally disabled and their families and siblings from birth to a point in time that they no longer inhabit this earth. The possibilities are endless; this could be a place where parents take their kids for therapy, early intervention, preschool, educational seminars on relevant topics, piano lessons, art class, warm water therapy – I could go on and on and on. Please fell free to use the next page to jot down your ideas for what this place would include; I will give you contact information later so you can send me your ideas. Write your ideas down now before they are lost or before you forget something that could impact thousands of lives:

If you are still having trouble grasping my idea, let me use my family as an example. Starting at two weeks of the boys' life, we started attending meetings held by Mile High Down Syndrome Association. At the time, these meetings were held in a church. Then at the age of six months or so, we started taking the boys to "therapy camps" – these too were held in a church. When the boys were two years old, we went to a preschool that specialized in working with the "special needs" kids and typical or normal kids; this school promoted integration of special needs into mainstream schooling. The curriculum included a mix of therapy and preschool materials. There are three different organizations involved in the aforementioned examples and these three places are in three different areas in Denver metro; so as you might imagine, we spent a fair amount of time in the car.

When the boys first entered into the school system, we provided transportation – during the elementary school years we walked; now in middle school the boys ride the bus. During most of the elementary school years we had the boys enrolled in private speech therapy which of course meant more time in the car. Now, at age thirteen, the only therapy or camps that we attend are in the summer for one week, which we gladly afford, as this is our "family vacation" during the summer school break.

Due to different interests on the part of the boys, we have not attempted Special Olympics or any other recreational type of program. The boys usually attempt to go in different directions and if Michele or I were to attempt, without the help of the other, to take the boys to any such activity, it would be as close to insanity as we could possibly get. So, we venture out very little and as a result, we have prevented ourselves and our children from living a more abundant life.

Looking forward can be grim, but it does not have to be; many families that are now where we will be at in four or five years have adapted to work, transportation schedules, meetings and so on. But what if... what if there was a place that offered everything that "The Trail" could offer and instead of compromising or just plain not doing anything at all, you could go to "The Trail"?

Imagine again as I use myself as an example: while Michele was pregnant, I would get up at 5am every weekday morning and go to the community recreation center and run for thirty to forty-five minutes. After the boys were born, I was too tired to get up that early and go exercise. Now, thirteen years later, my body looks like I get no exercise, but my mind knows that in order to stay alive at least as long as my children, I have to start getting some exercise. However, until I can find a way to do it without disrupting the harmony in my home and flow of income that we have desperately tried to create, exercise is, unfortunately, a low priority. Can you relate?

Again, I find myself facing the question, "Is this important and will it change people's lives?" The only answer I can come up with is yes. Furthermore, I hope that nonprofit organizations will office from this facility. Imagine again, if you will: you would like to gain some information about a therapy camp, but you are concerned about how long it will take and how your children will behave. Now how would this situation play out if there was a place you could go that would accommodate families with children that have special needs? Additionally, families with multiple children in which the siblings are typical or normal would find this place a welcome environment as well.

The Trail is a place for the entire family, a place for multiple nonprofit organizations to collaborate, offering services, recreation, employment, education and social activities; think of it as a mall for the developmentally disabled and their families.

Now for the best part: I am not proposing this idea so that I can earn a living from it, I am proposing this idea in order to build the facility, facilitate the nonprofit organizations and establish "The Trail" as a 501C3 nonprofit, complete with an executive director, necessary staff and a board of directors. How do I propose to fund this project, you ask? From the sales of this book.

Here is my plan thus far: the approximate size of the facility will be close to one hundred thousand square feet and cost approximately seventy million dollars to build; plus land, three million dollars and unexpected associated costs, twenty-five million dollars, for a total project cost of one hundred million dollars.

The sales of this book break down like this: at this point my projected profit per book is $10.00 if purchased at the retail price of $19.95, so in order to raise $100 million, ten million books need to be purchased. I know this does not sound easy, but it is realistic. It will be a lot of work, but all for a worthy cause; a community that deserves a better life with promise and value. In short: land, three million dollars; facility for the developmentally disabled, ninety-seven million dollars; better life for the developmentally disabled, PRICELESS.

How many books do I want you to purchase? One. Then tell everyone you know about this book and about the mission of the book, and ask each of these people to purchase one book for themselves and repeat what you just did. If you think you do not know enough people to make a difference, do what I do. As I write this, I have my sons' pictures on my keyboard at my office, every day, and I remind myself that they are worth me making a difference EVERY DAY.

Wondering why I selected $19.95 as the retail price? Kyle and Hunter were born in 1995; this is the year that I began to understand that everything matters, every day.

Closing Thoughts

To my dear wife, Michele: thank you for twenty-five years of marriage. We have been blessed with good times and bad, have been richer and poorer, have experienced both sickness and health. We have been blessed with our love for each other, a beautiful, strong friendship and two beautiful sons. I am blessed, privileged and honored to have you as my wife and best friend and I will love you endlessly, forever and ever.

When I have been at my lowest, you have lifted me up, given me confidence and been my biggest supporter. When I faced a staph infection that could have taken my life, you were strong for me and lifted me up. You ignore my many faults and love me for who I am; you make me a better person and my love grows for you each and every day. I sincerely look forward to the next twenty-five years.

To my mother, Emily: thank you for being my mother and grandmother to my sons. You were with Michele and me in the delivery room; having you live in our home has been both a blessing and learning experience. You have blessed me with your love, patience and support; I know there have been many times that I have disappointed you and I am grateful for your forgiveness. Chances are you will see my dad long before I do; please give him a hug from me and tell him I miss him every day.

To my father, Verdon "Pappy" Krei: I miss you every day. Someone asked me once, after I had become a father, what I wished for at Father's Day. I said I would like to be a father to my sons like my dad was to me, and if I could just do half as good a job, that would be more than enough.

My memory of you is still very clear, as is the fact that I attempt every day to make you proud and be the man you raised me to be. I look forward to seeing you again someday; until then, I appreciate you watching over me, Michele, Mom, Kyle and Hunter.

To my Creator and Heavenly Father: thank You. All honor and praise to You – in my life and in this book. You have created me in Your image and planned my destiny long in advance – thank You. For blessing me with the birth of Your Son, Jesus, and for blessing me with forgiveness and everlasting life, thank You. For blessing me with my parents, wife and sons that I may serve others in abundance, thank You.

In loving honor of my sons: Kyle Gene and Hunter Cole Krei.

Please contact author at:

kelly@kreilife.com

www.ingramcontent.com/pod-product-compliance
Lightning Source LLC
Chambersburg PA
CBHW060554100426
42742CB00013B/2557